On

Rusty Barnes

Nixes Mate Books
Allston, Massachusetts

Book design by d'Entremont
Cover photograph by Lauren Leja

Some of these poems appeared in the following journals,
Barn Owl Review, *Corium*, *Street Value*, and *Nixes Mate
Review*

Thanks to the following people and venues: Michael
McInnis, Ron Androla, Mary Biddinger, John Dorsey,
Heather Fowler, Nathan Graziano, Dave Roskos, Pressure
Press Presents.

ISBN 978-0-692-80593-0

Nixes Mate Books
POBox 1179
Allston, MA 02134
nixesmate.pub/books

for my father
Sherman Myron Barnes, 1935–2016.

Contents

On Broad Sound

Down Shirley Street

tonight is a banner night
all the folks are out
there's a killer light wind
sending the ocean smell
all the way to Bell Circle
two drug deals I interrupt
in front of the Cambodian
market while the Sound
throws up big waves I can
see stopped at the red light
at the bottom of the street
people pouring
into the subways. I want
pastries but get some
fake Twinkies at the Tedeschi's
instead. The fakies are OK
but like with breasts I prefer
the real thing and whatever
Shirley Street becomes at night
is more real than most.
Sometimes I get out of the car
just to smell it.

Beach Meditation

The beach lies fallow; dogs refuse to bark,
old Italian men, their bronze skin a landmark,

gossip in the native tongue while they ogle
the au pairs and young women who jog

by in their sports bras and hot pink earbuds
looking for the next phase of fitness by pounding

the asphalt; these early daylight hours soothe
me. I visit the pastry house at seven AM for

the day's ration of bread and tiny cannoli.
Sometimes the best part of the day comes

when I can hit the sand and look across
the gray water of Broad Sound toward England,

land of my father and forefathers. With
no small amount of Anglophile in me it takes

little effort to imagine myself there in
Cornwall or Wales with an out of-place

coonhound that craps wherever he wants on
the moor. Where I don't have to clean it up.

It's these small things that comfort me and my
queer habits: ricotta pie for breakfast,

that I don't understand a word of what's
going on around me on the beach

or in the bakery. I am a furriner wherever I
go, even in my Appalachian childhood home.

The sunlight seems tough here in Revere
and I don't have the stomach anymore to butt

heads with other men measuring their cocks
against some standard of behavior Neolithic

in its roots. I'd like to sit here on the bench
in the bakery till the skies shake down

around me and my soul enters the formless void
My dad told me this: Oblivion is no punishment;

it's just what I've come to understand after 45
years of expecting anything else to occur.

Heather at the Laundromax

How many nights? Working away the hours
between ten and midnight while I stayed

at home with the baby watching TV
trying to write something. You took

our loads of colors and whites
and threw them into the industrial-sized

washers and dryers that would no
longer take quarters. The vending

machines with detergent and bleach
and dryer sheets in variegated rows.

The Portuguese woman who ran
things folding the clothes of the well-

off who could afford the hefty fees,
the musical patter of the language

neither of us knew. I wondered then
if things would ever get better. Would

we ever reach the point where we
could have a washer and dryer? I

somehow envied you those nights,
surrounded by stories but having

worked all day before working more
at night I knew I had the easier time

of it and felt guilty. The sad sense I
tried to make then of the things you

did for love.

On the Blue Line Train
after Paul Blackburn

The light at night is two-toned shadow,
the car rocks gently to the side

round a curve that stretches one's
patience to the reeking point:

an old man asleep nearly topples
in place. The train carries me home,

busting a move into Beachmont
Station where some Latina lovelies exit

the train in high heels and tight jeans,
and I feel a horny fool for noticing them,

not much older than my daughter,
I immediately curse myself sad,

but I don't need to wonder why.
My bootheels clomp down

the escalator, that slow trip down
the steely machine. I'm always

afraid that, like my urges, someday
it will have its way: swallow me whole.

Luigi's Pizzeria (Best in Revere)

Some nights when it's beer o'clock
And my children are near-feral I like

To hit up the staff at Luigi's where
I can get a burger fries and beer

With the certain conviction like
Fresh mozzarella topping my mood

I will not find any better. I don't
Know anybody's name here and I

Have done this for years. They
Don't care who I am and I am

Comfortable not giving a fuck about
Who I am because they don't care,

And I love this about them. Like God
They. Don't. Care.

Revere City Hall

Traffic winds down the street,
Where a woman with a guitar
And a man with a washboard
Rake up a rhythm that hits
Me square in the pit. They
Don't know musicians don't
Play here because they prefer
The richer confines of Harvard
Square or Government Center.
I can imagine my father playing
His trombone blues with them
A slick player with a knack
For sounding fat in exactly the
Right place. But he's dying
Slowly four hundred long miles
Away. How can I mourn him
Now? He's a hair short of death
And I have nothing in my body
But his breath.

The Shipwreck Bar

I'm watching a drape-eyed girl,
callused fingers stretched
like paper over thin bones,
the star attraction in this bar
but this isn't one of those poems,
where there's some forlorn girl
and some hard-bitten guy
bouncing their tricks off each
other like quarters into an empty
shot glass or pumping each other
for information while her tiny
bare beach feet kick softly against
the runner. It's a poem about the
illegal bets being made all around,
the evening sun letting down outside,
and the bread-smell of Budweiser
in a cold long-neck bottle,
the scrape and craw of wooden barstools,
and most of all, it's about the way
the night negates possibility at the same
time the opportunities expand,
when that ship that's been creaking
on the wall seems to be coming in

again for you and for all your friends,
and it's about that drape-eyed girl
leaving the bar alone and walking
on the beach searching for stray kelp,
seeing a stray mutt,
and finding some old toy she left behind,
or something burning in the night mist,
something only she can know about,
something the world doesn't want her to have.

This Far

Just once I'd like to successfully
Piss my name into a snow bank

As an adult. They frown on that
Here in the city of Revere where

The potholes seem to be initialed
Off a list and forgotten about except

During election years when the elec-
Toral candidates want to impress

The residents at Orient Heights
And Beachmont. Mayor Dan Rizzo

Is a lovely man with whom I have
Shared cookies and cocoa at

The tree-lighting ceremony. I can't
Imagine asking him why I can't

Piss in the snow when the situation
Demands it. I just want a corner of

The yard to be mine in the way that
Any dog can mark his territory.

This is how far you can go, I want
To say to people. This far. No farther.

What God Knows and We Don't

Chicken kebab in the late afternoon sun
with the wind spritzing sand down my back

and the world made gloriously more real
by my wife and kids laughing among huge

crowds of beach people with over-dark
tans and the broad Massachusetts accent

I have come slowly to know as home.
Lifeguards cycle by relieving the shifts

of the others who get to try to drive home
through ribbons of streets marked off-limits.

It's an ordinary poem I write today
but I dedicate it to ordinary people who love

the salt and seaweed of the world and large
motorcycles spitting exhaust, the constant

pressure of a child's hand and a walk back
home up the hill dragging ass but knowing

tomorrow's payment for a good time will be
worth more than what we paid today, as

the horses at Suffolk Downs get farmed
out elsewhere so we do we get taken,

through the things we think we can't bear toward
the ones we can with the magic being that we

can't tell the difference between them.

Wonderland

opposite of what you might
expect provides no wonder at all,

but instead the red remains of a dog
track and a nearly empty stripmall.

They've built a suspension bridge
over Ocean Avenue like the Zakim

to help the commuters who ditch
their cars daily to take the Blue Line

into the city, the longest twenty
minutes you'll spend on any line

around Boston. Pigeons roost inside
the station despite the high-

pitched alarms built to save them.
No one can save the poor commuter.

After Sunday School, Winthrop Methodist Church

my son takes flight
there is no grace in him

only pure energy

my daughter beside him
spinning in loose circles

I want to wish them safe

the two of them in lockstep
always

but there is no safety

only my fears like vapors
woven into gods-eyes

and given back to me

The Marsh at Midday

Every time I visit the Belle Isle Marsh
I feel like a six foot two 300 pound target.
No crime takes place there that I can see
But any time I walk into the reeds I expect
to see a body or a rape taking place. Before
I had this feeling we buried my daughter's
dead hamster Brownie there under six
inches of loam and a rock pyre
in memoriam. My daughter didn't know
better so I went with my ace plan
at the burial: I recited from the Tibetan
Book of the Dead. O soul of Brownie
as you confront the endless void. . .
Then I forgot where I was and had to start
again at the beginning while inside I thought
Brownie you stinking offal in your expensive
cage I am reciting this because my daughter
does not know how to lose you and is chirping
back tears and even as I speak I do not
know how to lose her among these endless
alphabets of rock and starshine and tears
so I stand here in the marsh and gibber
silently to myself years after the fact in

this place I fear for both what it holds
and what may happen, neither of which
I can control.

Hichborn Street

is a right turn at the end of Winthrop
Avenue onto a long street: no outlet.
Police regularly patrol the area
for the black men and women who
break the speed limit just before
they make the left onto Route 16.
I stalled out there on a dark night
in December once and one of those
targeted men unlimbered himself
from his car and jumped my engine.
I shook his hand and offered him
ten bucks he wouldn't take. The next
time I saw him the newspaper said
he'd been beaten with a ball bat
until his wife didn't recognize
him. I felt empty and shocked as if
somehow I'd caused his mishap by
not being there when he needed a
witness. I can only repay him by
paying it all forward and wishing
that night he'd been beaten that
the panacea of my participation
might have saved both of us.

Lamp

A street lamp lights the way in the fog
like a torch in the steam from the sewer pipes.

Along the way three homeless men huddle
around a barrel fire as a cop draws nearer.

This is my adoptive city my second home,
even filled as it is with tourists and students,

but I can see Broad Sound from my window
and on a clear day some of the harbor islands

from the stony beach near our house where
dogs shit illegally and play with their criminal

masters and the bums get the rush twice
a week. It's a short steep walk back up

the hill to the modest house we purchased
the first major investment of our lives

and the lamp that I steer by now is you.

Peter's Super Beef

The man at the counter barks
my order to the grill guy in Greek,

as I wait for my chicken parm
sub and some fries. Peter's

Super Beef is packed with dinner
orders to go, working class to the hilt.

I'm forty-six and I look like a college
poofter compared with the muscled

guys making their way in here for
cheese steaks and onion rings.

I like to grab my shit quick and eat
at a table near the tiny rest room

where I can watch these workers
with their t-shirts and dirty jeans

standing three deep at the counter
talking about the Pats game,

still in their hard hats and tool
belts. They all remind me of my

old man washing the grease off
his hands with Goop and getting

a beer out of the Coke machine
at work before driving me home after

baseball practice. I watch one man
in particular – his hair in a jarhead

buzz – order a steak bomb,
not the way my old man got

it at home with onions on his
Minute Steaks and plastic-wrapped

cheese. It's 1977 all over again,
except I paid for my own stuff.

I get to watch as these men
bond over the greasy food.

I think of my old man this way:
alive, with dirt under his nails.

Meditation at Dunkin Donuts

I order the same thing
every time,

but what I really want
is conversation.

Twice a day
I enter and get my iced

coffee (extra cream and
sugar) to overhear

Regina talk & shovel
cubes into my cup

as Alessandro rings me up
and tries to sell

me a gift card for
a friend, he says.

I don't have the heart
to tell him

I don't have any.

I Love You, Satori

On a bus to the Northgate
Shopping Center I'm stuck
next to a porcine transit
cop. Every button on his
uniform strains. I wonder why
he's there. Then I realize
it's not fat it's a Kevlar jacket
under his clothes. I feel badly
for a moment because I am fat.
I go out the folding door.
A swallow delicately sips
from a puddle. I am still fat.

Moon Pie

Sitting in Torretta's bakery all the men
around me speak in Italian to the owner
where I simply sip my coffee and pretend
to tear into their ricotta pie. I wonder what
they could be saying and if the Mafia
rumors are true. At the next table my kids
are puzzled as rooster without hens.
Why don't they speak English? my youngest
asks. While I'm thinking of an answer my
eldest steps in. Because they're more comfy
that way. My youngest sagely nods and goes
back to her moon pie.

On Traveling the Northeast

Only one-horse towns like pills
on a sweater. I prefer them.
The blue highways and the
green forest show the way
A spot on the map grows
larger by the Google search.
At home the water chops out
in Broad Sound and seahorses
sing us to sleep.

Point of Pines 9/11/16

Gulls lift on the breeze.
This isn't a nature poem.

We are illegally
parked and laughing it off,

trespassing on the private
beach, low tide pushing kelp

against the gray sand,
where a dog barks,

chases its tail,
runs headlong toward

our car,
pisses on a tire.

A house near here
boasts exactly forty-five

American flags. I
look up and see

a plane showing
its belly as it lands

at Logan,
all passengers intact.

The horror I see
is in my own mind.

Suffolk Downs

The handlers exercise horses in the dawn hours,
Thousands of pounds of marvelous beasts whose

Hooves clatter down the dirt track like shoes
Thrown down the stairs until the handlers catch

The rhythm of the horses and the sound becomes
Words when even the hardcore gamblers pause

In front of the simulcasts to listen to the hoof-noise
Of these tremendous bodies of skill and grace,

The tickets being punched and the money being
Dealt all stopping as the old men in faded green

Khakis and hoary eyes wait in vain for one
More winner while the number three horse

Puts them in the money and they celebrate,
backhanding the man next to them in the chest,

Hoping against the gods that they'll win just
One more time before checking out for good.

Torretta's Bakery

Old men drink espresso
In tiny paper mugs

Like medicine cups

While outside on the veranda
In wrought-iron chairs

Their wives talk,

La moglie di mio figlio è terribile,
Awful, one says.

Puttana, says the other.

She holds up her water bottle,
Red fingernails gleaming on

Her wrinkled hand.

The Blue Line train thunders by
On its way

In another country entirely.

Would You Like Some Cake?

Two nights ago I sat in the Dunkin Donuts
parking lot stealing their wifi and tippling

an iced latte and a man in a dun half-shirt
opened my car door sat down and said

you look like a bear.

His hair twirled round his neck like water
runs downhill pooling at his bare clavicles.

Aren't you a little cold? I said. He said no
it's balmy here would you like some cake?

I did not know that the menu featured cake.

How delightful, I said. I will eat cake with you.

He reached into his backpack and pulled out
a cupcake which he carefully cracked

in pieces offering me the large share. You
bears, he said. You're always so hungry.

Here. You eat the other piece too the man
said, thrusting it at me.

You're a beautiful

man he said. I hope to see you again in my
dreams. He revealed

his broken mouth to me

and left the car. and I went home and ate
my nice dinner, held off dessert

thought deep thoughts about bears.

Belle Isle Marsh

stretches across a heavy swath
of real estate in Revere. People

walk their dogs here and gay men
cruise the lonely old buggers

whose sex lives are spent on
their knees late at night when

the danger is more palpable. During
the last month two men have

been attacked here. It is quiet
enough today, dogs everywhere,

shit on every unwary walker's
shoe though the gimlet eye

of a police officer takes
the measure of every man

to see if he presents a danger.
I let the kids run ahead of me

laughing and playing tag amidst
the reeds. This is what they know

of freedom. How can I spoil it?

Loneliness

From my deck I can see Boston
in the wintertime buildings rising
to the clouds through snakebitten
trees: that overlay of dark blue sky.

I see nothing in the summertime
which makes sense to me. Trees
show green like a mime's scarf,
the people pollution rots the city

like ditch weed rots your lungs
but still I sit here with my Kindle
linking me to the greater world
and feel lonely. Nothing

feels like loneliness and lone-
liness feels like nothing. I have
a family secreted in the house
like birds in a hollow tree nest.

Solitude is one thing I like but
loneliness is another thing.
The way I love my family breeds
it in the open spaces of my being.

It's hard to confess it now but
like engenders like and sometimes
I catch my wife or kid with that same
look in their eyes--distance and

sorrow--and I want to press them
to my chest and believe in
that old saying about seeing forests
for trees. That look we give

each other when nothing's right
and we beg to see through
branches or our own hearts or
see things clearly: see anything at all.

Northgate Shopping Center (a rant)

Don't go there in a snowstorm,
the piles of snow will go higher
than your car and every clueless
git thinks he or she
can navigate it. For a bunch of New
Englanders these fuckers can't
drive to save themselves, 4-Runners
rocketing off into the side
of the McDonald's drive-through
motherfuckers in KIA's sliding like ducks
on ice with everybody driving the
wrong way up the lanes next
to the CVS. All I need is the med-
icine I have to have to operate
in this world to begin with. What
I want is the sweet neck of your
average beer bottle. I'd stick my
tongue down its glassy throat
for just a hint of oblivion.

Nobody Wins

I'm standing by liquor store on Winthrop
Avenue with four feet of snow in a city
with an attitude problem I'm going
to cure with peppermint schnapps.
Across the way the Dunkin Donuts fills
with stragglers like lonely starfish
waiting for the 450 bus to the Northgate
Shopping Center. I wait for the bakery
to be done with the afternoon pies
so I can pick up some luscious ricotta.
My kids are good, my wife will be home
soon then a guy comes out of the liquor store
and throws a bunch of scratch tickets
at me. Nobody worthwhile ever fuckin wins,
he says, but I've pissed out the signs
of my future into the dirty snow and cardboard
piled by the side door. It looks OK, for now.

The Poet John Wieners

I once saw John Wieners declaiming
poems in a soft but strong voice out-
side the Harvard Gardens in the rear
corner of the Back Bay. It had to be

near midnight and at that point I
didn't know he was John Wieners
he was another homeless nut in
a city filled with them. We'd gone

outside for some air but my compadres
and I quit our jiving around
and listened to him recite a poem
I can only claim to witness as a tiny

poetic moment in his life. He didn't
know me which is fine as poets don't
have to reveal themselves to me just
because I want them to in my poem.

We listened at the bar as the man
made our drinks. I happened to be
drinking only Kamikazes then. I
didn't really know anything else

to order besides rum and coke
and beer. My 2nd year of grad school
kicked the country boy out of me
in these social situations. I didn't

know what I was doing there but John
Wieners always knew what he was
doing. He was a poet whatever company
he was in. I'm still learning that now

twenty-two years later as I knock
back rye and think of an old man
reciting his works to a bar full of
stupid kids like me. Goddamn it.

I should have bought him a drink.

What Can We Do?

On being told sharks see dark skin better than white
  (unverified)

Tonight even the hand puppets in Congress
are wordless in the wake of fires in the West

while sand sharks swim the tidal pools on Revere
Beach looking for the dark-skinned people

because apparently sharks see darkness better.
Who would have thought? Take the way great

whites bite anything in sight; infinitely preferable
to the ones who seek out dark skin even if it's

a scientific fact because we don't have to explain
to our children why black men standing idly in front

of ritzy hotels are subject to tackle and handcuff
with no constraint against renegade cops (they

can't all be like that can they?) or the bellwether
impact of radio talk show and heated subway debate.

When my kid looks up at me (not for long, I know)
and asks me why cops do this/why people do this

and I want to give him the liberal handjob I've been
given my entire adult life I find I cannot do it any

longer. Listen kid, every man out there is out there
seeing how he can get his genetic material prop-

agated. He doesn't have any idea why any more
than the shark does. It's the way he was raised

because people of color are other and the white man
doesn't want to hear about other; like a forest fire

white anger against brown is the modus operandi
and to go against that is to deny years of exposure.

The truth is those dark men and women are no more
dangerous than any other but the burning rage

of the forest fire when compared to the slick
chicanery of the shark is beyond the idea that

most whites can believe. The fire is out there con-
flagrating and the sharks are out there taking in

the buffet of all colors. Truth be told neither one
of them can be stopped. They can't even be con-

tained temporarily. The loudness of the majority
always overcomes, the biggest shark always wins

and the forest fire consumes everything in the
path but for the few humans willing to fight it.

Bell Circle at 4:30 PM

A round-robin of delivery drivers,
the people clinging desperately
to their nearly-wrecked cars,
the jaywalking pedestrians,
those often broken traffic lights,
all the nausea-inducing bicyclists,
the check-cashing storefront,
that shit-poor Pizza Hut,
the feral cats that scatter
across the road like rats
dumped from a Capitol Waste
truck filled with day-olds
from the Dunkin Donuts
close by, but this – this Bahamian
woman, a vision in tight shorts
and a bathing suit top strutting
with her baby carriage makes
me look twice and then again
before my wife smacks me
in the chest bringing it all back
home from where I've been
traveling, far away from Revere.

What You See on Shirley Street

A woman pushing a child crosses
the street from BK's Bar to the beach,

pushing the child by the butt like
a dog and dragging a cheap stroller

behind her. I didn't know you
could even bring kids into bars,

so already this day has taught
me something. The street also

teaches: buy pot here not heroin;
the Cambodian market is less

easy to scam than the bodega;
hang out here long enough you

might see a good tattoo; there's
a satellite police station on the beach.

but no cop is ever there. What the
street seems to want us to learn

is that every story you see here
has four sides and if you listen

closely you can hear them all
under the pavilions and on the wind

with the smell of cheap hot dogs
and the ever present sea air.

SeaWitch Restaurant, Peabody MA

Look your lobster lunch in the eye,
and try not to show your disdain

for the crowd of old ladies talking
loud shit about whatever comes

to mind, including credit card fraud,
Southern accents, the price of tea

at the local convenience store,
the way those Pakis run their

businesses. Smile as your wife
grimaces and your children bend

to their shrimp with red faces. Dear
God, even the children are embarrassed

by these women, who have nothing
positive to say. Listen closely as

your son says, for real, Dad?
Are they for real? And you stammer

and try to tell them what
the world is and what it takes

sometimes to be the better
person, to walk away without

calling them out on their shit.
Never look a gossipy old lady

in the eye.

The View from Earth

If you were in space and you looked back
my love might be the biggest thing you see.

Fuck that Chinese wall and the trails
of Conestoga wagons in the midwest,

you could look just south of anywhere
and witness the mass of shooting clouds

and the triphammered horn of my heart break-
ing the bowl of soup the sea has become.

It says to you don't leave don't fly away
the things you part with as you leave earth

matter just as much as asteroids which shake
off pollen and continue on their merry way toward

planetary destruction, just ask the Tungusku
forest how nothing will grow in the impact

crater that is more like a radioactive no-fly
zone but what I'm saying is don't die love

ever: make it so the cosmos knows your name
shoot it out in big bright lights so that when

you look at Alpha Centauri and feel that bigness
and muchness, come back to little earth. Look for

the guy standing next to the ocean in Revere
Massachusetts, the big one with the gray beard

and the perfect children and watch as he pledges
to give you everything all over again if he can

if you don't leave and he don't leave and the oceans
stay wet you might stand to see another lifetime

as codfish or snappers or even the tiny amoebas
tickling the anemone or giving the shark another

remora to support. The point is he said don't wink
out like a star but be with me again and again.

About the Author

Rusty Barnes grew up in rural Appalachia but has lived in East Boston and Revere, MA for the past twenty years with his wife, poet Heather Sullivan, and their family. He's published his work in more than two hundred journals and anthologies. His poetry chapbooks include *Redneck Poems* and *Broke*, and his full-length poetry collection, *I Am Not Ariel*, appeared in 2013. His latest novel is *Ridgerunner*.

Nixes Mate is a tiny island in Boston Harbor first used by colonists to graze their sheep. The island became infamous after the bodies of convicted pirates were gibbetted there to serve as warnings to mutinous sailors.

Nixes Mate Books features small-batch artisanal literature, created by writers that use all 26 letters of the alphabet and then some, honing their craft the time-honored way: one line at a time.

Forthcoming titles from Nixes Mate Books:

KINKY KEEPS THE HOUSE CLEAN | Ash Deweese

WAR IN THE TIME OF LOVE | Michael McInnis

nixesmate.pub/books

Made in the USA
Coppell, TX
01 March 2021